NEW HORIZONS

IN AMERICAN ART

WITH AN INTRODUCTION BY HOLGER CAHILL

NATIONAL DIRECTOR · FEDERAL ART PROJECT

THE MUSEUM OF MODERN ART

NEW YORK · 1936

REPRINT EDITION, 1969
PUBLISHED FOR THE MUSEUM OF MODERN ART BY ARNO PRESS

Copyright, September, 1936, The Museum of Modern Art, New York

Reprint Edition, 1969   Arno Press
Library of Congress Catalog Card No. 75-86428

CONTENTS

FOREWORD

This exhibition of work done under the Federal Art Project of the Works Progress Administration is intended to serve as a visual report to the public: a documented survey of one year's activity. In certain respects it is of necessity incomplete. Murals, decorative sculpture and various other types of work produced on the Project are unsuited to museum presentation. A great deal of work worthy of inclusion could not be shown because of lack of space. Despite these limitations, the exhibition can justly be called comprehensive. The material, assembled from every section of the United States, has been selected by the director of the exhibition for its artistic value alone, no effort being made to consider it from a regional aspect. Taken as a whole, apart from its interest as an index of individual talents, it reveals certain major trends in contemporary American art.

The Museum acknowledges with thanks the invaluable assistance of Miss Constance Rourke and Mr. Holger Cahill, National Director of the Federal Art Project, in the preparation of the catalog.

ALFRED H. BARR, JR.

NEW HORIZONS IN AMERICAN ART

When the long view of American art is taken it becomes clear that the American artist has rarely had a full and free relationship with a public or with his own time. The cleavage has become increasingly apparent under the stress of social and economic uncertainties which have faced the American artist sharply since the middle of the nineteenth century, and which have faced him with tragic immediacy in recent years.

American art has always been extremely sensitive to cosmopolitan ideas, and throughout its history has responded to rapid waves of influence from abroad, but the breaks and changes of which one is so conscious in art have not been due simply to alterations in European styles or techniques and our response to them. Far more deeply they are the result of disturbances in the relationship between the artist and his public. Changes in art theories, in styles and techniques, draw more force from the social environment than most art historians are willing to admit. The course of social change, accelerated at certain periods, retarded at others, has always been registered in art. In the recent past there has been a great deal of talk about new forms, but the artist has always made use of whatever forms are available, modifying and altering them to meet new situations. Art is a normal social growth deeply rooted in the life of mankind and extremely sensitive to the environments created by human society.

There is a theory that art always somehow takes care of itself, as if it were a rootless plant feeding upon itself in sequestered places. Many people are willing to believe, in a time like this, when art patronage has dwindled to infinitesimal proportions, that it is not necessary for organized society to do anything in particular, because no matter what happens, a few artists starving in garrets will see to it that art does not die. It is quite obvious that this theory will not hold. Consider the case of Colonial and early Republican portrait painting. Looking at the work of men like Feke, Copley, Earl, and Stuart, one might assume that the excellence of early American portraiture is due simply to the fortunate fact that these talented men happened to be alive. What would have become of these talents if the landed aristocracy and the rich merchants had not been equal to the event, if there had been no sound tradition of art patronage, no social interest in portraiture and no active demand for it? The answer is supplied by history.

Social and economic changes early in the nineteenth century put an end to the greatest portrait school this country has produced. When the landed aristocracy which had dominated the eighteenth century was superseded by the beneficiaries of the industrial order portrait painting declined. And as photography came into general use toward the middle of the nineteenth century—along with the general spread of the print—our great portrait tradition entered a twilight zone from which it could not be rescued, not even by the prosaic honesty of Eastman Johnson, the incorruptible integrity of Thomas Eakins, the technical skill of Duveneck, or the extraordinary virtuosity of Sargent.

During the latter half of the eighteenth century and the first decades of the nineteenth, public appreciation of art was dominated by the Colonial tradition of good taste which in its latter phases tended to make of American art no more than a tasteful resumé of earlier European practice. Yet, during this long era, native strains definitely appeared. The period between 1820 and 1870 was far more provincial—and so in a sense more genuinely American—than the eighteenth century had been. Into the cultural life of the eastern seaboard came the upsetting spirit of frontier democracy, brushing aside in many localities the earlier, more aristocratic tradition and creating a new homespun quality in American art. One might say that American art was renewing itself through new contacts with the American earth and the American people. The frontier was unfolding; population was growing rapidly under the stimulus of industrialism. It was the day of Andrew Jackson and Davy Crockett, of frontier democracy and the rise of the common man. It was also the great period of folk and popular art. The level of taste drifted toward the provincial-popular.

ART AND THE COMMON MAN

The interests of the common man began definitely to shape American art in this period, particularly through the medium of the print. Perfection of new processes of printing and engraving resulted in hundreds of publications, which in turn furnished a market for illustrators who could depict the American scene and American racial and social types. Prints could easily be circulated throughout a large country in which the means of transportation were still limited. Even the backwoodsman often possessed almanacs in which woodcuts and line engravings appeared. Colored lithographs, such as those of Currier and Ives, appeared everywhere. Prints exerted an influence not only upon the popular appreciation of art but also upon the the ideas and techniques of artists.

Further, in the paintings of the popular scene, in the landscapes of the Hudson River school, and in the panoramas of the painters of spectacular landscapes, the public found an art which had a genuine use. It formulated and stimulated ideas or sentiments concerning people and places, which were of value in the social and political development of the nation. With the exception of certain Europe-trained painters and a group of sculptors who were busied with Italianate imitations, most of the artists of this period were thus in harmony with dominant interests of their age. If their taste was not always of the best, it was an honest taste, a genuine reflection of community interests and of community experience.

LOSS OF SOCIAL CONTEXT

After the Civil War the picture changed completely, and American art began to be subjected to disintegrating forces which have been active up to our own generation. The rapid expansion of industrialism made for the dominance of social groups which had no tradition of art patronage and little interest in art except as it might serve as the badge of a newly-acquired social distinction or as an object of conspicuous display. Roger Fry and other writers have observed that whenever a situation of this sort arises its associated phenomenon is usually that of extreme vulgarity in taste. After the Civil War the new generation of art patrons demanded the grandiose, the vulgar, the spectacular, the over-embellished, and the over-genteel—this last as a means of obliterating their crude beginnings. Archæology and astute dealers supplied them with art objects which had somehow been associated with grandeur in the past and which were still associated with the taste of the socially powerful in Europe. The American patron turned to esthetic fragments torn from their social background but trailing clouds of aristocratic glory.

The serious result of this wasteful showiness was less the spread of vulgarity than the dislocation of art in this period from its social context. In a society with such aims there was little place for the creative artist whose concern was with the expression of human experience. Faced with social indifference and dissatisfied with the techniques and ideals of their craft as they were then practiced in this country, American artists were compelled to seek a healthier environment elsewhere, and often sought this in Europe. The question of Henry James, "Is one's only safety, then, in flight?" was answered in the affirmative by many American artists. Whistler, Mary Cassatt and a host of others fled to Europe. In America, Albert Pinkham Ryder drew about him the cloak of the solitary; Thomas Eakins suffered almost complete isolation and neglect; and Winslow Homer, one of the few major artists who found public support in his generation, in the end withdrew from it.

CHANGING CONCEPT OF NATURE

The first really serious breach between the American artist and his public had occurred. This breach gradually widened to the point where the artist virtually lost contact with his social environment, and his plight became more difficult because he was influenced by profound changes, taking place in the latter years of the century, as to concepts of nature and its relation to art. Throughout most of the eighteenth century and well into the nineteenth the concept of nature had served as a unifying element in literature as well as in the fine arts. Nature had been conceived as a principle underlying the forms and phenomena of the visual world, drawing them into a harmonious and purposive whole, benevolent and somehow friendly to man's interests and ideals. Art had been conceived as a harmony dependent upon the harmony of nature.

Thus for a long period nature provided a satisfying relationship for the artist, giving him a sense of continuity and completion. This conception of nature as a unifying force is implicit in the painting of the Hudson River school and in the work of such men as Ryder, Homer, and Inness. But these were the last American painters of major stature in whose work appears any measurable echo of this romantic conception. In their later years, toward the end of the nineteenth century, art in this country was swept by a movement which meant a radical alteration in basic attitudes. This was French Impressionism. Recognition of the fact that a conception of nature was no longer a unifying element in art was implicit in Impressionist methods. Nature was no longer a harmony to be studied. It became something that furnished occasions for the exercise of a technique. The new attitude was carried to much greater length by the Post-Impressionists and was explicitly stated by Paul Cézanne, who said that "art is a harmony paralleling that of nature." Art, in other words, had its own harmony, independent of nature. This idea was carried to its final term by the Cubists who declared that art need have no frame of reference in nature at all. The relationship with nature, which had given the artist a creative impetus for upward of two hundred years, thus tended to disappear.

THE ISOLATION OF ART

Since the human element had already been banished there was nowhere for the artist to turn but to art itself. In content and idea, as well as in style and technique, the source and the center, the unifying element for art was henceforth to be art. From the close of the nineteenth century to the very recent past art has been feeding on itself.

This tendency did not mean simply a perverse insistence that art should be created only for art's sake. It was a recognition by artists that they no longer had deep roots in nature or in human society. The situation was not of their own making. It was part of a general pattern of dissolving loyalties and relationships brought on by the rapid advance of industrial civilization and by the break-up of romantic conceptions under the impact of modern science.

In a fashion it was a reflection of the good sense of artists that they refused to wander in a void, brooding upon their loneliness and isolation They had made a fresh move. By a natural transition they turned back to historical sources and explored European traditions, studying these in the light of Oriental and primitive art. In Baroque, Renaissance, Medieval,

stepped into the situation American art would enter a dark age from which it might not recover for generations. It was to meet this situation that the United States Government established a series of art projects.

THE FEDERAL ART PROJECT

The Federal Art Project, which is represented in this exhibition, was set up in August, 1935, by Harry L. Hopkins, Administrator of the Works Progress Administration. This Project has thus been functioning for a little more than a year. It took over a number of small state projects operating under the Federal Emergency Relief Administration and unified them under a national program. Most of these state projects had developed under the Public Works of Art Project, established by Mr. Hopkins as part of the Civil Works Administration program in December, 1933. This earlier project, known popularly as PWAP, was administered by the Treasury Department under the direction of Edward Bruce. It came to an end in June, 1934.

When the present Federal Art Project was organized, about one thousand of the original thirty-five hundred artists who had worked under PWAP were employed on various undertakings in several states. The number of artists on relief was approximately four thousand, and it was clear that something like fifteen hundred or two thousand others, not yet on relief, were living on the margin of subsistence. Today, approximately fifty-three hundred artists are working on the Federal Art Project, which is directed by a small staff in Washington. Artists, museum directors, and art teachers in public schools, colleges, and universities have been chosen to act as advisers in the field and as state or regional directors. Others from the same professional groups are acting on voluntary committees, and have been of the greatest service in stimulating local interest in the art program and in helping to maintain high standards of excellence.

ART AND GOVERNMENT SUPPORT

Because of the many activities undertaken by the Federal Art Project, the United States Government has become the greatest art patron in the world. The number of artists engaged is not large when the size of the population and the area of this country from coast to coast are considered; and government support for art is no new phenomenon. Governments in every age and in every part of the world have employed artists. Egypt, Greece, Rome, many of the city and provincial governments of medieval and modern Europe, governments in China and other Oriental countries, as well as the ancient civilizations which flourished on the American continent, may be cited as examples. The great building program in Athens under Pericles, which left an imperishable record of Greek civilization, employed large numbers of artists, artisans, and craftsmen on government projects.

In our own time, the French government has long had a liberal policy of encouraging art and public education in art, as have Italy, Germany, Russia, and other European countries. In Sweden a finely planned art program has been established, leading to an outstanding development of the industrial arts in that country. Government support of art was undertaken in a striking fashion in the 1920's by the Republic of Mexico. A group of Mexican painters was commissioned to paint murals for public buildings under the direction of the Ministry of Education. From the work of that group came an art movement which spread through the country and far across its borders, carrying the fame of Mexico to every part of the world.

CONSERVATION OF SKILLS

Conservation of the nation's resources has in our time become a major function of government. Under the Federal Art Project the conservation of artistic skills and talents has been a primary problem. It was a vital necessity that all types of talent should find forms of expression suited to their special aptitudes and abilities. It is a mistake to suppose that all of the large body of artists working on the Project were in normal times devoted to the fine arts or that they have all been set to work indiscriminately under the Project on easel paintings, murals, or sculpture. Slightly less than one half of the total number employed are working in the fine arts. The others are craftsmen, workers in commercial and applied art, and in some cases are what might be called journeymen painters or sculptors of useful if not outstanding talent.

The organization of the Project has proceeded on the principle that it is not the solitary genius but a sound general movement which maintains art as a vital, functioning part of any cultural scheme. Art is not a matter of rare, occasional masterpieces. The emphasis upon masterpieces is a nineteenth century phenomenon. It is primarily a collector's idea and has little relation to an art movement. When one goes through the galleries of Europe which preserve, in spite of war, fire, flood, and other destructive forces, an amazing quantity of works from the past, one is struck by the extraordinary amount of work which was produced in the great periods. During the early part of the twentieth century it is said that some forty thousand artists were at work in Paris. It is doubtful if history will remember more than a dozen or two of these, but it is probable that if the great number of artists had not been working, very few of these two dozen would have been stimulated to creative endeavor. In a genuine art movement a great reservoir of art is created in many forms, both major and minor.

FINE ART AND ART FOR USE

European critics have always recognized the usefulness of the minor artist of excellent but not necessarily creative gifts; he has often made contributions of great importance to the art movements of his time, notably through educational or historical undertakings. The contribution of the craftsman or worker in the practical arts has also been recognized. It is clear that in the best periods of art expression the homely crafts and the fine arts have been closely integrated.

In organizing the Federal Art program the many forces which tend to build up a sound art movement have been considered. An effort has been made to view American art in perspective, both as to the past and as to the future. While the fate of the workers in the fine arts has seemed of paramount importance, it is clear that under the most favorable conditions these artists cannot prosper alone, nor can they by their solitary efforts create a fully developed art movement in America.

The importance of an integration between the fine arts and the practical arts has been recognized from the first by the Federal Art Project, as an objective desirable in itself and as a means of drawing together major esthetic forces in this country. Our manufacturing system has produced much that may be called good from the esthetic point of view, but it has also produced a fearful clutter of unlovely things, and this in turn has resulted in a degradation of popular taste, since these objects provide the only art that many individals know. Direction from the fine arts has been sorely needed for the manufacturer, the craftsman, and the public. It has been impossible to provide a solution for all the ensuing problems under an emergency program, but an attempt has been made by the Federal Art Project to break down the artificial barrier which exists between these forms of art expression. The young commercial artist has received direction, which has often been distinguished, from teachers or workers in the fine arts. In the printshops and workshops set up under the Project, in the making of posters, mural maps, dioramas, lantern slides for schools, of scenic models for natural history museums, young workers in the fine and the practical arts have come together to work out mutual problems. The outcome has been the accomplishment of many useful services for public institutions, and a stimulation toward higher levels in the creation of objects of common use. (Numbers 382-391.)

THE YOUNG ARTIST

As these workers under the Project have been organized, still another group has received special attention. The problem of the young artist of distinguished but still emergent gifts has been of major concern. If American art is to continue, the talents of the younger generation of artists must not only be encouraged but must be given an opportunity to develop. Under the Project arrangements have been made by which the experienced professional artist has directed the work of groups of young workers in the fine arts. Something like the master-pupil relationship of the Renaissance has developed as these groups have worked together, with the result that the young artist has benefited by the experience of the mature professional, while the professional in turn has been exposed to the constructive influence of that responsibility. Many professional artists have testified as to the interest and stimulus provided by this relationship.

An important gain has been the breaking down of isolation which has almost habitually surrounded the mature artist in this country, and a broadening of social relationships.

For the young artist another relationship has seemed of importance. Because of the development of local or regional creative or teaching projects, the young artist has tended for perhaps the first time within the modern period to attack the problems of art at home, in his own setting, among familiar surroundings, in the midst of a social life which he is likely to know well. This situation—part of it enforced by the depression—has meant at least a beginning toward a naturalization of art in all our communities, an outcome which must be achieved if our art is to be anything more than an effervescence along the Atlantic seaboard.

The rise and abundance of young talent throughout the country has been heartening to all those connected with the Federal Art Project. Yet a definite challenge has been heard from a few quarters as to its development. Why, it has been asked, should young artists be encouraged to continue in the field of art if over-production already exists in that field? It is true that the studios of many of our gifted, older artists are filled with unsold paintings and sculptures. But the crucial circumstance is not over-production in art; rather it is under-consumption. As has been suggested, a comparatively slight possession of art exists in this country today. Few people own art, yet the potential audience for American art is extremely wide. As new publics for art develop—as they seem bound to do—our supply of artists may actually prove to be too small. Even now there are signs of this. A far wider demand for works of art has developed on the part of schools, libraries and other public institutions than the Federal Art Project, with its large body of workers, has been able to meet. "Our schools are bare." "We have no art of any kind in this community." Appeals containing statements of this kind are constantly being received by the directors of state and regional projects. One school superintendent has declared, "The art teachers in our schools have never had an opportunity to see an original work of art." This last may seem incredible, but it is true not only that many teachers of art have been entirely lacking in such opportunities, but that courses in art are being given in teachers' training colleges without

20

the use of any original works of art whatever. The Federal Art Project has repeatedly been asked to help remedy this striking deficiency.

An attempt to bridge the gap between the American artist and the American public has governed the entire program of the Federal Art Project. At many points, as we have seen, the lack of a firm relationship has resulted in uncertainty and even disruption in the sequences of American art. Under the Project popular art, in the best sense, has seemed highly desirable. Critics have sometimes suggested that popularization involves vulgarization, but this is not necessarily true. Vulgarization usually occurs, as in the Gilded Age, when groups seeking to rise in the social scale use art as an object of conspicuous display. The general public of the present day is not concerned with these objectives. Experience under the Project, as this has developed throughout the country, has shown a sincere response to art, a genuine demand for it, and a widespread popular interest. The problem has been to meet this popular concern by the best use of the available talent.

EXPERIMENTAL GALLERIES

It is not too much to say that people in whole areas of this country have had little or no experience in art. The channels have not been created by which art could reach those who wish to enjoy it. Many states in the South, the West and the Middle West, for example, have been almost entirely lacking in art galleries. Under the Federal Art Project, since January, 1936, the experience and talent of artists on relief have been utilized to establish and direct nineteen experimental art galleries in the South with the purpose of breaking down these great disparities in opportunity. These galleries are located in the Carolinas, Tennessee, Alabama, Virginia, Oklahoma, and Florida. They have been visited by nearly half a million people during this short period, and many other proofs of a genuine popular response have become clear.

In arranging exhibitions for these galleries emphasis has been placed upon the work of local or regional artists; in many instances no general opportunity to see this work has existed. Painting and sculpture from other and often distant parts of the country have also been shown, including works created under the Federal Art Project. Contemporary art has thus been brought into an active, popular, regional interchange in many places for the first time.

Important phases of community interest have also been studied and utilized in arranging exhibits. In Chattanooga the manufacturing background of the city has been taken into consideration. In Big Stone Gap, Virginia, the pioneer arts and crafts which form a link between the past and the present have been shown. In Mobile, interesting collections which had lain in storage for twenty years have been brought to light and have been made to form the nucleus for a permanent museum. In Greenville, South Carolina, plans are under way for the establishment of a textile museum, allied with the major industry of the district. In North Carolina and Tennessee, special thought has been given to exhibits of local crafts which will attract and hold the interest of people from the mountain sections.

All these new galleries are situated in central downtown sections where people may drop in easily, and most of them are kept open until nine o'clock in the evening to permit workers to visit them. Many persons come who would hesitate to enter large and imposing museums. Friendliness and informality mark the programs. Lectures or demonstration talks by artists or teachers on the Project, illustrating the use of the various art media, have revealed art as a form of enjoyment, not as a hard intellectual struggle for which an expensive and specialized education is required. Many individuals are learning for the first time to read the language of painting. One director has set up her own art library in the corner of a gallery, lending the books to those who care to use them, with a consequent widening of interest and knowledge.

TEACHING AND CHILDREN'S WORK

The classes in painting, modelling, carving and weaving, which have been formed in these southern galleries, are typical of an important section of the Federal Art program. No phase of its work is of greater social significance than its teaching. Hundreds of highly trained teachers of art, displaced by depression economy, are holding classes daily in boys' clubs, girls' service leagues, in schools after hours, in churches and settlement houses. Several thousand persons have joined classes in the southern galleries. In New York City and its vicinity fifty thousand children and adults are being reached weekly through the teaching force of the Federal Art Project. A widening area of social influence has been created by the classes for under-privileged children, taking them off the street and providing fresh and natural outlets for expression. One school superintendent has stated a typical conclusion, saying that these classes have "done more to stabilize the schools in this city during a difficult period than any other single agency." Educators and social workers have also emphasized the larger public understanding of art which has developed from these classes.

The work of children in art classes under the Project has attracted a considerable amount of attention, and is included in this exhibition as an integral part of the Federal program. These children are taught through practice rather than by verbal instruction, each child being given training in the craft of the art and then allowed to develop his own personal expression. Intensity of feeling has produced instinctive simplifications in their painting and sculpture. Most of the city children know little about nature and paint it infrequently, while children in the smaller towns of the South and West turn to it spontaneously. A large proportion of these youngsters are realists, describing their impressions of speeding locomotives, of steamboats, and of El trains undaunted by detail or compositional complexity. A butcher shop, a Passover scene, "Yentas" bargaining over fish, a drugstore where ten cents will buy a banana split, are some of the subjects which they have described with a bold vividness sometimes denied to adults. (Plates 392-427.) In sculpture they have shown themselves unafraid of their materials. They do not seek beautiful surfaces or prettiness of detail but let their sense of the round and the flat, the crest and the hollow, pass directly into the material. (Plates 428-434.)

Among the settlements and community houses where this work has been accomplished are the Hudson Guild, the Boys' Welcome Home, the Gramercy Boys' Club, the East Side Jewish Settlement in New York, the Avery Memorial in Hartford, Connecticut, Friendship House and the Americanization School in Washington, D. C., and centers in Michigan,

Tennessee, Virginia, and other states. The general age range of the children taught under this program has been from eight to sixteen, though many younger children have been included. It has not been expected that all or even a large proportion of these children will develop into professional artists, but the high quality of much of their work has its broad suggestiveness as to the wide spread of unconscious talent; and there can be no doubt that this work tends toward the development of a greater sensitiveness to art among this coming generation. These young people will form a genuine audience for American art in the future.

INDEX OF AMERICAN DESIGN

With these many orientations, the Federal Art program during the past year has striven for a sound accomplishment based upon a distinct consciousness of the problems of the future. An effort has also been made to consider the past. American artists and designers have always lacked the sense of continuities which well-defined traditions can bring. Even with our recent vigorous research many of these traditions have not yet been uncovered—they are not yet a firm body of reference. So far as both the past and the present are concerned, the artist has constantly met the challenging question whether there is such a thing as American art. It has been possible for many artists to say that the hunt for a usable American past is a vain one, with the implication that the artist takes off only from the immediate present, and that the only unifying principle in art today is the loyalty of the artist to his craft and to the styles and manners of expression which have been the vogue in the contemporary era. This point of view has been due mainly to recognition of the fact that, aside from its European heritage, American art lacks the bedrock of a classical past. Its history does not exhibit the continuities and progressions which give a firm impression of order to the history of Old World cultures, an order enhanced for our American perception by the sentiment of distance and the foreshortening of time.

The search for a usable American past in the arts is not a simple one because of the weight of European influence and the many breaks and changes in American art itself. However, it would be a mistake to believe that a summing up of outside influences defines the character of American art, or that its history is, in the main, the story of a cultural lag, as so many students would have us believe. Naturally such difficult research and interpretation as are required to establish clear perspectives in this field cannot be completely carried out under an emergency program. This is the special task of critics or groups of critics. Yet it has been possible to turn the talents of many artists on the Project toward an undertaking which will, it is hoped, make a positive contribution in this direction.

The Index of American Design, now well advanced in twenty-five states, and comprising a large series of portfolios, will depict the decorative arts in America from their inception well through the nineteenth century. For at least a hundred years and in many instances for a longer period, artists and designers in Europe have recognized the importance of such compilations. They have been considered as important, not by any means as a basis for imitation but as a wellspring to which workers in all the arts might turn for a renewed sense of native traditions in design. In Europe these compilations have frequently been published by government subsidy, so great has been the value attached to them.

In this country nothing of the sort has been attempted up to this time. Excellent special studies have appeared, but these have often been limited in scope, limited in the material upon which they could draw, limited also in their study of the material considered in relation to tendencies in design in other fields. One of the results of the work of the Index will be the opportunity to trace alliances between the many forms of decorative arts that have appeared in different and sometimes widely separated parts of the country. Already striking interconnections, not always to be easily explained, have been shown, as between certain patterns in embroidery designs from New England of the seventeenth century, in the Shaker inspirationals of the 1840's and 1850's, and again in some of the chest paintings and santos of the Mexican border.

American decorative arts as shown in furniture, costumes, embroideries, textiles, coverlets, ironwork, ceramics, glass, silver, pewter, toys, as revealed in architectural details, weathervanes, wood sculpture for decorative purposes such as ships' figureheads and shop signs or other related crafts, local or folk arts such as scrimshaw, form the basic materials for the Index. Artists on the Project have made record drawings in color for the most part, but photography or black and white have been used when color is not important. Both public and private collections have been drawn upon for the selection of significant or beautiful examples, and every phase of this undertaking has been accompanied by adequate research, bringing to light both objects and the circumstances of their creation which have not hitherto received attention.

All this work has been done under the direction of supervisors, trained both in the history of the decorative arts and in their adequate representation. Experts outside the Project whose knowledge is unquestionable have been untiringly generous in giving their services when advice or assistance has been needed. The Index has received from them, as from many others, enthusiastic support.

Not least of the phases of interest stirred by the Index has come from the artists who are creating it. High standards have been set for their work, and they have collaborated in maintaining these. Many groups have formed classes in order to perfect their technique and to study the history of the objects which they are depicting. The artists at work on the Index are drawn from all sections of the Project, from those who have been accustomed to devote themselves to the fine arts, and those who have worked in the commercial field. Through this work many young artists have learned techniques which will prove valuable to them in later years.

There can be no question as to the indirect returns for the artists engaged in this undertaking. They are placed in a constant relationship with fine forms, with objects of great intrinsic interest or excellence in design and workmanship. They have become aware of the decorative sequences which these objects represent. These are by-products of the work of the Index, but they must be considered important by-products when the development of American art as a whole is considered. Many of these artists are frank to say that their study of these objects represents their first contact with the arts of design of earlier periods in this country.

Inevitably, in this connection, the question arises whether these rich decorative materials are genuinely American. Are they not derivative, all of them? Is the native element strong? Ernest Fenellosa has admirably said that "alien influence is invariably at the heart of the native development." Japanese art contains an altered composite of Korean, Chinese, and other Asiatic forms. English portraiture of the 17th and 18th century stems from Dutch and Flemish masters. Yet distinct changes have always taken place as the older or alien forms have become rooted in new soil. In this country such transformations have often been strongly marked. The stripping down to a few essentials demanded by colonial life; our early limited means for manufacture; the rigorous, practical, unadorned existence of the earliest settlers had a determining effect upon their adaptation of continental forms. As the work of the Index has proceeded, fresh and distinctive groupings, definitely American in character, have been shown in a wide array of materials. The extent of these groupings will best appear in the full scope of the Index.

Certainly it is clear that the decorative arts which have developed on American soil are important for American designers, not only because they are American but also because they preserve fundamental human and cultural values. They are also important for the worker in the fine arts, since these forms represent the esthetic language popularly spoken through decades in many parts of the country. In the furniture and textiles of the Shakers, in the ceramics of the Pennsylvania Germans, in the iron work and pottery of the southern states have appeared striking phases of native esthetic development. These and others will continue to have much to say to the designer, student, and critic.

At the present time approximately thirty-five hundred plates in color have been completed. An ensuing problem is that of adequate reproduction at a moderate cost, so that art schools, public schools, libraries, colleges, and universities, may acquire sets of the portfolios. In New Mexico a portfolio of Spanish-Colonial Index plates is being reproduced by means of key block linoleum cuts, combined with hand-coloring. Reproduction of this character is, of course, necessarily limited. What is desirable, if the work of the Index is to come into active use, is a fairly inexpensive form of mechanical reproduction. At the workshops of several of the Index units experiments are now under way as to the use of the color lithography process for printing the Index in sets of portfolios for museums, libraries, and schools. Plans for publication on a broad scale are now being considered. In the meantime, admirable plates are steadily accumulating in many parts of the country. These will represent a permanent body of invaluable work, which can be deposited in museums where artists and students may have access to them.

THE FINE ARTS PROJECTS

Naturally in any program of this kind the position of the creative artist has been considered as of primary importance. If the main stream of American art is to continue, he must be given a chance to develop and to assume the leadership which belongs to him in a sound general movement. An art tradition may be said to have existence only as it is created anew by each generation. No matter what the museum collections tell us about the past it is in the work of present-day artists that we must look for the living tradition.

That the tradition of American art is still vigorous is amply shown by the response of creative artists to government encouragement and support. This response has been magnificent. Their production has been large and of high quality. They have worked with intelligence, energy, and initiative.

While the marked rise of the young artist under the Project is not its only significant development, this tends to show that the Project has performed a genuine function in permitting and encouraging the growth of new talent. Of the artists on the Fine Arts Projects represented in this exhibition sixty-four are under thirty years of age. Many are in their early twenties. Recognition of the importance of this young talent has been received from many quarters. While prizes and fellowships are in themselves relatively unimportant they are evidence from outside the Project of the high quality of the work produced. In the mural field, one Project artist was awarded the gold medal of the Architectural League, generally conceded to be the highest honor in decorative painting in the United States. A painting by one artist was purchased by the Metropolitan Museum of Art in New York; another was purchased by the Phillips Memorial Gallery in Washington, D. C. Three artists have won prizes at the National

Academy of Design; four at the Cleveland Museum's Annual Show. Three have won Guggenheim Foundation Fellowships, and one a fellowship at the MacDowell Colony.

A full and free expression on the part of creative artists may have come about in a measure at this time because of a release from the gruelling pressure which most of them suffered during the early part of the depression. It seems to have its origin also in a special set of circumstances determined by the Project. The new and outstanding situation is that these artists have been working with a growing sense of public demand for what they produce. For the first time in American art history a direct and sound relationship has been established between the American public and the artist. Community organizations of all kinds have asked for his work. In the discussions and interchanges between the artist and the public concerning murals, easel paintings, prints, and sculptures for public buildings, through the arrangements for allocations of art in many forms to schools and libraries, an active and often very human relationship has been created. The artist has become aware of every type of community demand for art, and has had the prospect of increasingly larger audiences, of greatly extended public interest. There has been at least the promise of a broader and socially sounder base for American art with the suggestion that the age-old cleavage between artist and public is not dictated by the very nature of our society. New horizons have come into view.

American artists have discovered that they have work to do in the world. Awareness of society's need and desire for what they can produce has given them a new sense of continuity and assurance. This awareness has served to enhance the already apparent trend toward social content in art. In some instances the search for social content has taken the form of an illustrative approach to certain aspects of the contemporary American scene—a swing back to the point of view of the *genre* painters of the nineteenth century. Evidences of social satire have also appeared. In many phases of American expression this has been no more than a reaction against the genteel tradition or a confession of helplessness. The dominant trend today, as illustrated by the Project work, is more positive. There is a development toward greater vigor, unity, and clarity of statement, a search for an adequate symbolism in the expression of contemporary American experience, less dependence on the easily obvious in subject matter, and a definite relation to local and regional environments.

The fact that the Federal Art Project has made it possible for hundreds of artists to work in their home environments has led to interesting developments in many parts of the country. Heretofore certain regions have been barren of art and art interest because of a constant drift of talent toward the already overcrowded art centers in the East. The Project has helped to counteract this movement. One result has been that a great deal of latent local interest has been brought to the surface and stimulated into healthy activity. Another is that many little-known aspects of this extraordinarily varied country of ours have been brought into the current of art. Through this we are discovering that the country differs considerably from the "standardized America" which was so thoroughly advertised in the recent past. There has been no attempt under the Project to foster a "regional art," assuming that a regional art is possible in this day of easy transportation. But art that is related to the history or the local color of a region has been encouraged where this has seemed a natural expression for the artist.

What strikes one about the Project work in general is relevance to contemporary life and sound technical knowledge. In every section of the country there are honest, vigorous, and independent artists whose work has the firm discipline and intelligent craftsmanship which give assurance of solid achievement in the present and stimulate high hopes for the future. The period of experimentation and research through which artists have passed in the last twenty years or more has given them a technical equipment of great range, and has made for high standards of performance. This technique is no longer being used simply for technique's sake. It is being turned to vital and useful ends in searching out expressive forms for what is most positive and valuable in the unfolding experience of the American community.

MURALS

It is known that wall painting in one form or another has been practiced in this country since the eighteenth century, at least. Most of this work, especially in the early period, was of the provincial-popular type. It was done probably by the itinerant limners who were a feature of American village life up to the middle of the nineteenth century, and many of whom may still be found today, especially in the South. Up to the third quarter of the nineteenth century, most of our better-known murals, like the paintings in the dome of the National Capitol, were the work of European artists.

From 1876, when John La Farge began to decorate the interior of Trinity Church in Boston, there has been a recurrent interest in the mural among American artists, with 1893, the year of the World's Columbian Exposition, standing out as a sort of minor peak of popularity. The best of this nineteenth century work is unquestionably that of John La Farge. Since his time, there has been a good deal of mural painting in this country, but not until the past decade has there been anything resembling a general movement.

In recent years a revival of public interest in mural painting has been stimulated by the work of Thomas Benton and Boardman Robinson, by the veritable renaissance of the mural art begun under the Mexican Government Projects in the 1920's and by work done in this country by the most prominent exemplars of this movement, Diego Rivera and José Clemente Orozco. Since the beginning of the 1930's, American interest in mural painting has increased to a remarkable extent. The exhibition of designs by thirty-five painters and fourteen photographers at the Museum of Modern Art in May, 1932, focussed for artists and public alike the problems and the possibilities of the mural art.

In the following year Harry L. Hopkins set up the first large government art project under the Civil Works Administration and gave American artists an opportunity to practice the mural art on a scale commensurate with their abilities and aspirations. Since that time the development has been continuous and dramatic. Private patrons, convinced by the results achieved under the government program, are turning to the mural with increasing interest since they have before their eyes the proof that American artists are using the medium with understanding and authority.

It is significant of contemporary trends in American art that so many

31

of the artists working on the Project have submitted themselves to the discipline of a severe medium. Mural painting, and especially painting in true fresco, does not permit the individual variations possible in oil or watercolor. The problems of fresco painting are extremely complex. The painter must know exactly what he wants to do with the space, and have a great deal of knowledge of the chemical relationships of various materials, especially of the relationship of mortar mixtures to colors. No matter what the medium, whether fresco, secco, tempera, or oil, the mural technique has certain possibilities and limitations which the painter must respect. The mural must have definite relation to its surroundings and be an integral part of an architectural scheme. The color, the scale, and the character of the painting must harmonize with the color, scale and character of the surrounding architecture. The composition as a whole must have clarity, largeness, carrying power, and a rhythmic order that leads the eye easily through the whole space. Mural art is suited to large, simple forms, and its color schemes are much more severely limited than those of the easel painter.

Many sketches, a great deal of research, and the hardest kind of purely physical labor must precede the actual painting on the wall. During the painting the artists usually work in public places where people congregate. Mural painting is not a studio art; by its very nature it is social. In its great periods it has always been associated with the expression of social meanings, the experience, history, ideas, and beliefs of a community. There is no question that the work here presented clearly indicates an orientation in this direction. (Numbers 8, 13, 44, 47.)

Since it would be impossible to include murals which have been painted in fresco directly on the wall, and since even the transportable murals lose much of their significance apart from their setting, it is difficult to give a complete picture of this phase of the Federal Art Project work. However, even the necessarily limited selection of designs, sketches, details, models, and photographs in this exhibition offers a fairly comprehensive picture of accomplishment and promise.

It is significant that a large proportion of the murals produced under the Federal Art Project during this first year are by young artists. These artists came to maturity at a time when mural painting, because of government support, was no longer a dream. The country was asking for murals. The many problems involved, problems of large space, architectural limitations, technical complexities, the handling of subject matter, were a challenge which the artists accepted. Courage to meet these problems was born of opportunity.

The work here exhibited gives positive indication that American artists have a mural sense and that they have gone about their work in this field with enthusiasm, independence, and directness. A variety of styles has developed, but the murals have in common a feeling for monumental construction, for design control, for rhythmic balance and inter-relation of parts. The treatment shows that many of the artists have achieved a real mastery in this art which is relatively new to them. The handling of subject matter is usually both imaginative and appropriate; the medium selected the most sympathetic to the space and the subject. Throughout the country one sees a spontaneous interest in local source material. This is true of the eastern group, and it is particularly true of the western and middle western mural painters, many of whom are unknown in New York. These artists may be called regionalists in that they turn naturally to themes linked with the life, landscape, and history of their regions. There is, however, nothing here of a false localism or of a romanticising of the past. (Numbers 24, 32, 49.)

During the first year of the Project 434 murals have been completed, 55 are in progress, and sketches are being prepared for a great many others. These murals are requested by public institutions which defray material costs. It is a most encouraging sign that, in addition to the murals already mentioned, there are hundreds of requests for others. In every section of the country there are waiting lists for Federal Art Project murals. It is not too much to say that this work, as it develops, gives promise of a truly monumental art which will express with honesty, clarity, and power the experience and ideas of American communities.

EASEL PAINTING

The largest number of creative artists engaged on the Federal Art

Project are working on easel pictures in oil, watercolor, tempera, and pastel. Some of this work is done in central studios where groups of artists work together, but most of it is done in the studios of the artists employed.

Evidence of a recovery of social context is clear in the work of the easel painters, but it is natural that this should be less striking than it is in the work of the muralists. The development of the easel painter's techniques, especially that of oil painting, is associated with the rise of individualism in western Europe. From their beginnings these techniques have been directed toward refinements and devices which would enable the individual artist to use the greatest freedom in expressing subtle nuances of personal statement and variations in style and expression. In the oil medium the artist is in almost complete control of his material, to an extent unknown in sculpture, for instance, where the character of the material is obviously resistant. As a result, particularly in recent years the tendency has been toward over-refinement and intricacy of personalized expression to the point of rarification.

Emphasis upon technique for its own sake may not have entirely vanished from the work produced on the Project, but a strong tendency away from it has become apparent. The modest but essential virtues of honesty and freshness have developed. Perhaps the most heartening feature of the highly varied easel painting on the Project is its comparative freedom from imitative entanglements, the absence of anything which might be called hero-worship. There is very little in this work which follows fashionable reputations at home or abroad; no residue of the point of view which in the past has tended to make American art a tasteful resumé of European practice. In view of the great influence of the van Gogh exhibition at the Museum of Modern Art last winter it is interesting to note that the work under the Project has conspicuously failed to echo either the design or the color of this master. The influence of the School of Paris is rather slight. With the decline of dependence on outside influences, preciosity and self-consciousness have tended to disappear. These artists have come to see that preciosity is related to the worship of esthetic fragments torn from their social contexts, and to the idea of art for the select few. The lack of self-consciousness may be an expression of American naiveté. But when one

34

considers the "fearful progress in self-consciousness" which Jacques Maritain observed in contemporary painting, this change alone is a clear gain.

An outstanding characteristic of the easel painting under the Project has been the initiative in meeting new problems, coupled with an admirable command of the several media used. These artists have been making their own free and confident assertions. Figure painting and still life have interested them very little. Few studio subjects have appeared. This new work is often close to the quick, spontaneous life which is at the artist's door—which, at least, he now perceives to be at his door.

A marked decentralization of art expression may have turned many painters toward wider perspectives and a consideration of more immediate subjects and materials. This decentralization has been inevitable as artists have been forced by the depression to remain in their home environments. Regional differences have come into play, in the Far West, in the Southwest, in New England. The skies of California, the quiet spaces of middle-western farming country, the remoteness of a fisherman's shack on the coast of Maine are a few instances of a true exploration which has little or nothing to do with personal idiosyncrasies and a great deal to do with personal expression in a profound sense. A fresh poetry of the soil has appeared, with a marked freedom from formula.

Whatever else may be said about American painting in the past, however uncertain may have been its direction, an honest literalism has been developed in nearly all periods. In some phases, as in the work of Eakins, this literalism has been pushed by a severe integrity to the point of genius. Except for the remote magnificence of Ryder, the strain of poetry has been less clear. It must be admitted that emotional values have not been strongly sustained in American art of the past. The Project artists represented here have realistic integrity, but they are not overly interested in literalism, and a good deal of their work, whether it has to do with portraiture, landscape, the social scene, or pure fantasy, indicates a reappearance of emotion in painting with very little trace of the personal exoticism which has characterized much of the romantic painting of the recent past. "Imaginative realism" may be used to describe this tendency, a realism which means a genuine recovery of emotion.

35

SCULPTURE

Compared with other sections of the Federal Art Project, with easel painting, for instance, the sculpture representation in this exhibition is small. This proportion, however, is a fairly accurate reflection of the comparative popularity of painting and sculpture in our time. The opportunities for the development of sculpture in the contemporary period have been limited. The controlling factors in this situation are lack of demand for sculpture in connection with architectural plans and the almost exclusive interest of museums and collectors in archaeology. No popular demand for sculpture has been created because the collectors' desire for rare pieces has led to the custom of limiting casts to a small number with the result that prices have been too high for the average man.

Roughly, one may divide sculpture into the architectural, the civic or commemorative monument, portraiture, and the figure. Excellent portraits and figures have been produced in this country since the days of William Rush and John Frazee, who may be considered our first sculptors. The monument has seldom offered much to the creative artist. The greatest opportunity for sculpture, it would appear, should be in the architectural field, but these two arts, so closely united in classical antiquity and in the Middle Ages, have followed divergent paths in the modern period.

Considerable demand for monumental and architectural sculpture appeared in this country after the middle of the nineteenth century. At that time our sculptors, coming out of a period of imitative neo-classicism, were developing a more romantic trend which emphasized pictorial quality, naturalistic treatment, and a lively handling of surfaces. These qualities are excellent in the portrait and even in the figure but they are not suited to the architectural and monumental.

In the past generation American sculptors have given a great deal of thought to the architectonic. But during this same period the architects, pursuing functionalist tendencies which developed in the nineteenth century, were carrying to its logical term an architectural style denuded of sculpture. A reaction against this tendency has taken place in recent years, both in America and in Europe, and architects are now trying to include sculpture in their plans. Significant attempts to relate sculpture to architecture have been made in government buildings in Washington, in various government housing units such as First Houses (Plate 254), and at Rockefeller Center in New York. There has been considerable use of relief sculpture on façades, of relief and free sculpture in pediments and interiors. It does not appear that all these efforts have been successful. The important thing is that they have been made; that there has been a sincere attempt to unite the distinct but related arts of sculpture and architecture.

It is evident that sculpture will not find its place in the life of our time until a harmonious relationship with architecture has been established and until a popular demand is developed through a wider distribution of casts at a moderate price. For these reasons the greater part of the Project sculpture has been designed to harmonize with architectural plans, and to stimulate a demand for sculpture in public buildings. Many friezes, pediments, plaques, panels, and figures have been installed in schools, colleges, libraries, government housing units, and other public buildings. A good deal of the free sculpture on the Project has been designed to fit specific locations in public parks, botanical gardens, and courtyards of buildings. (Numbers 256, 256.) Many casts have been distributed to schools and libraries. (Number 257.)

Because so much of its work is in the architectural and decorative fields very little of the Project sculpture is available for exhibition. The examples here shown, however, illustrate certain broad contemporary tendencies. The first thing that strikes one is the general high level of technical accomplishment. Due to the marked improvement in American art teaching since the turn of the century, and to the experiment and research which artists have been carrying on for the past generation, sculptors now have a technical and stylistic equipment of great range. There are many working on the Project who are thoroughly expert in all branches of their craft, in modelling or carving in relief or in the round, as well as in casting. It is a healthy sign that in spite of all this technical equipment there is very little interest in virtuosity, in the manipulation of surfaces to give an adventitious impression of liveliness, or in easy decorative effects in the handling of silhouette or drapery. Instead there is, in general, an honest and unpretentious approach, and an acceptance of the essentially sculptural idea that this

37

art involves a collaboration between the artist and his material. From the point of view of style one notices a comparative freedom from the archaeological bias, from the eclecticism of the recent past, as well as from the literalism of the nineteenth century. There is very little of the classic idealizing tendency which has been so popular in American sculpture, and which, in many ways, is a heritage of the genteel tradition with its emphasis on "seeing beautifully." There is a definite interest in the architectural foundation of sculpture, in rhythm and design, the relation of form and space, in mass, and movement. There is a new emphasis on architectural appropriateness and decorative purpose. The growing interest in human significance should serve not only to bring the sculptor into closer touch with the life of his time, but also to stimulate wider public interest. It seems reasonable to believe that, through the work of the Federal Art Project, a great many people, coming into daily contact with sculpture, will be trained more effectively in the understanding of an art which, except in its more illustrative phases, has always seemed difficult to the general public.

GRAPHIC ARTS

Prints have been both a popular and important phase of American art expression since the 1830's, when the interests of the common man began definitely to influence American cultural life. Toward the close of the nineteenth century they suffered a decline because of the cheap commercialism which followed the great success of Currier and Ives, and also because the perfection of photo-engraving made possible an entirely new pictorial world for the American public.

As the popular interest declined, the collector and museum official directed their attention to the medium of etching. Particularly since Whistler's time, and until the present decade, the etching maintained its hold in the affections of the print connoisseur, and nearly every major American artist tried his hand at this medium. Many distinguished plates were produced in this country, and great virtuosity was developed in technique. But vitality was sapped, and the creative element dwindled as false values came to be established through preciosity. The rare replaced the fine work of art. Accidents in printing, often deliberate, created "special states;" the size of editions was reduced; and collectors as well as museums paid record prices for rarity and a display of means rather than for quality or content. Thus the audience became smaller and smaller, and with the exception of the few truly creative etchers, most print makers in the opening decades of the twentieth century turned to the freer and more democratic medium of lithography.

Graphic art history shows that each period usually has a predominant interest in one medium. Since the late 1920's lithography has been emphasized. Every general print exhibition since that time has shown lithographs. The character of the medium offers a minimum of technical problems and arbitrary limitations. The public has quickly responded to the rich variation of tone, subtle color suggestion, dramatic contrasts of light and dark, and the great variety of subject matter which have appeared in lithography. Popular interest grew very rapidly. The print was taken out of the precious portfolio and brought into the intimate environment of the home. Special editions in large quantities were produced at prices within the range of the average purse. The cause and result both contributed toward a concentration on lithography.

Today, on the Project, an extraordinary versatility has come into being. Not only lithography but every known branch of the graphic arts has its practitioners. Encouragement to technical experiment, the supply of needed materials and well-equipped workshops, have broadened the field so that in this exhibition we find a most comprehensive diversity of media, often treated with real mastery: lithography, lithotint, color lithography, etching, aquatint, wood block, linoleum cut, colored wood block, and wood engraving. Each artist has been free to select the medium most sympathetic to his vision. It is of special significance to note how inclusive is the choice of the artist, and how the interest in such comparatively difficult media as wood engraving has progressed. The variety of treatment, and the skill with which these techniques have been handled, are illustrated in the collection of prints shown. (Plates 192, 193, 203, 216, 228, 239.)

As might be expected from its history in this country, the print is extremely sensitive to the contemporary environment, and is an art rich in social content. It would almost be possible to reconstruct a social history of

39

our period from the prints produced on the Federal Art Project. The prints give a fresh and vital interpretation of life as it is lived in America today, and give first evidence of new directions. Every aspect of the American scene is reflected, the cities with their medley of architectural styles, skyscrapers, bridges, interiors, gasoline tanks, factories, subways, railways, airplanes, harbors, farms, cabins, wheat fields, mountains, mines, sports, politics, racial and social types, the whole kaleidoscope of American life.

ART AND SOCIETY

No complete picture of the program of the Federal Art Project can be given in a museum exhibition. Much of its work, such as murals, decorative sculpture, stage sets, and various types of visual aids for educational purposes, is not suited to museum presentation. The teaching program, which has had wide implications, can be only suggested. The character of this work has been determined by public demand for art, and it has been designed to meet specific needs and locations as part of broad educational plans.

Yet the works shown in this exhibition indicate important phases of a year's accomplishment. From the point of view of the artist and the public they have a significance far beyond that of the record, beyond even their value as individual works of art. Taken as a whole they reveal major trends and directions in contemporary expression, and a view toward new horizons. Surely art is not merely decorative, a sort of unrelated accompaniment to life. In a genuine sense it should have use; it should be interwoven with the very stuff and texture of human experience, intensifying that experience, making it more profound, rich, clear, and coherent. This can be accomplished only if the artist is functioning freely in relation to society, and if society wants what he is able to offer.

The idea which has seemed most fruitful in contemporary art—particularly as shown by the work of artists under the Project—has been that of participation. Though the measure of security provided by the government in these difficult times unquestionably has been important, a sense of an active participation in the life and thought and movement of their own time has undoubtedly been even more significant for a large number of artists, particularly those in the younger groups. A new concept of social loyalty and responsibility, of the artist's union with his fellow men in origin and in destiny, seems to be replacing the romantic concept of nature which for so many years gave to artists and to many others a unifying approach to art. This concept is capable of great development in intellectual range and emotional power. This is what gives meaning to the social content of art in its deepest sense. An end seems to be in sight to the kind of detachment which removed the artist from common experience, and which at its worst gave rise to an art merely for the museum, or a rarified preciousness. This change does not mean any loss in the peculiarly personal expression which any artist of marked gifts will necessarily develop. Rather it means a greater scope and freedom for a more complete personal expression.

It is fortunate that, under government auspices, an opportunity for the development of significant new tendencies has been provided during these crucial times. The outcome is full of promise for the future. Certainly there is no dearth of genuine talent in this country—talent of a rich order. Under the most difficult circumstances American artists have shown themselves ready to attack new problems and to make fresh adaptations. They are growing in stature and in power. They have the technique, the discipline, and the impulse to carry American art to new heights. The question for the future is whether they may continue to maintain that sound relationship with a wide public which has been shown to be essential for a living art.

HOLGER CAHILL

PLATES

MURALS

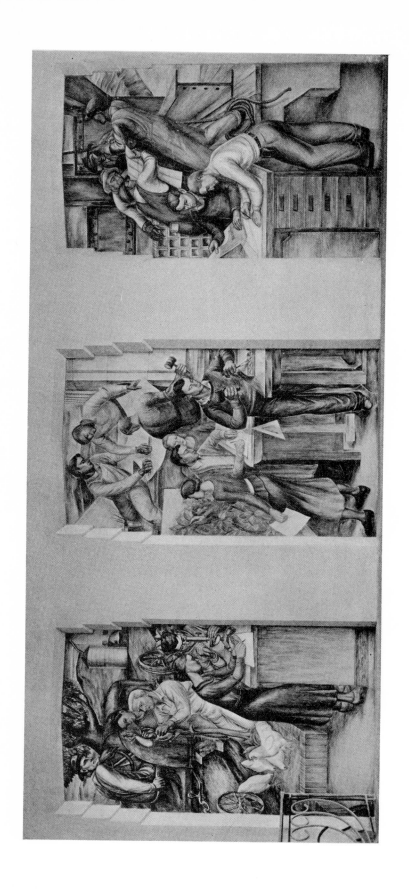

8 Edgar Britton, Illinois: Classroom Studies and Their Application
Three completed panels of a series of six

8 Edgar Britton, Illinois: Classroom Studies and Their Application
One completed panel of a series of six

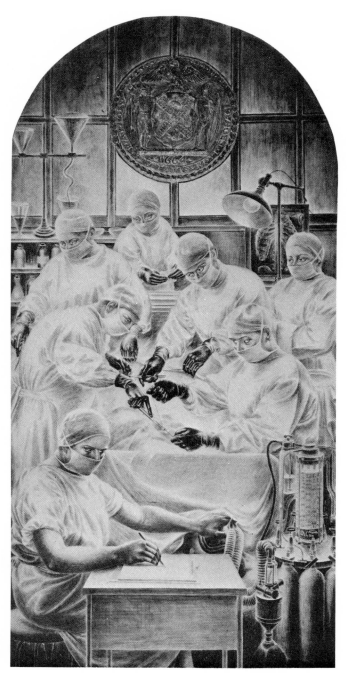

13 Alfred Crimi, New York: Preventive Medicine and Surgery
Completed panel

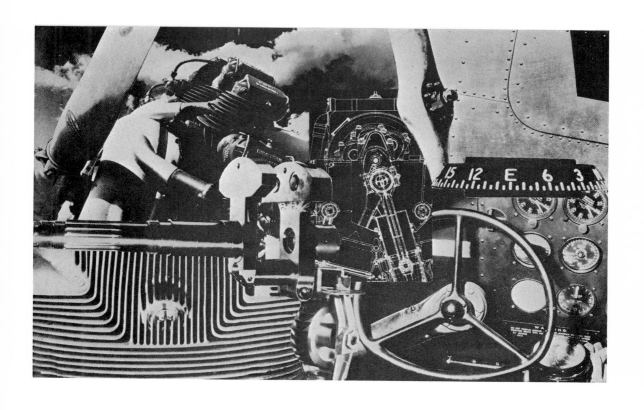

14 Wyatt Davis, New York: Mechanical Aspects of Airplane Construction
    Study for photo-mural

23 Ralf Henricksen, Illinois: The Elements
Watercolor study for two of four panels: Earth and Water

42 Hester Miller Murray, Illinois: World of Children
One completed panel of a series of three

24 Emanuel Jacobson, Illinois: Early Schoolroom
Watercolor study for one of a series of panels

32 Karl Kelpe, Illinois: Pioneer Days
One of two completed panels: Early Farmers

28 Edwin Boyd Johnson, Illinois: Medical Pioneers
    One completed panel: Head of Pasteur

51 Max Spivak, New York: Puppets
One completed panel of a series of nine

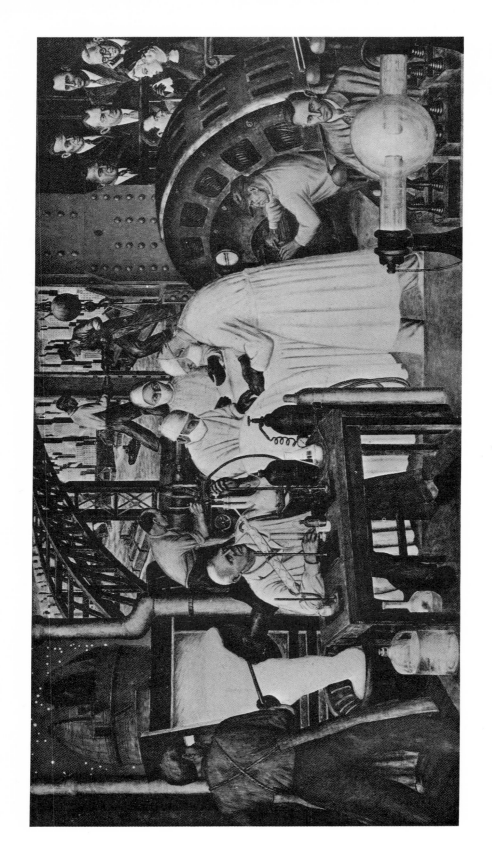

44　James Michael Newell, New York: *Evolution of Western Civilization*
One completed panel of a series of five

44 James Michael Newell, New York: Evolution of Western Civilization
One completed panel of a series of five

49 Mitchell Siporin, Illinois: Prairie Poets
Tempera study for proposed fresco

48 Anatol Shulkin, New Jersey: Historical and Social Function of the Court
Tempera study for one of four panels: The Need for the Law

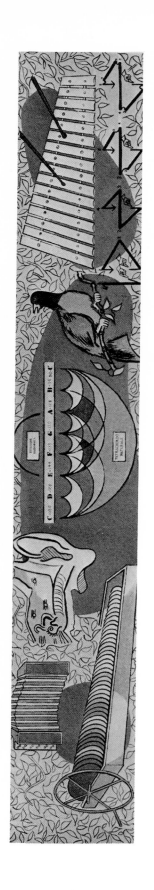

35 Karl Knaths, Massachusetts: Series of panels in a school music room
Two completed panels

EASEL PAINTINGS

70 Pedro Cervantez, New Mexico: Croquet Ground

73   Joseph De Martini, New York: Moonlight

74 Emmet Edwards, New York: Abstraction

76 Karl Fortess, New York: Winter Vista

77 Leon Garland, Illinois: Fry Street

84 Leon Kelly, Pennsylvania: Setting the Table

79 Louis Guglielmi, New York: Wedding in South Street

87 Lawrence Lebduska, New York: Farm Team

91 William Littlefield, Massachusetts: Fantasy of a Fire and Figure

90　Jack Levine, Massachusetts: Conference

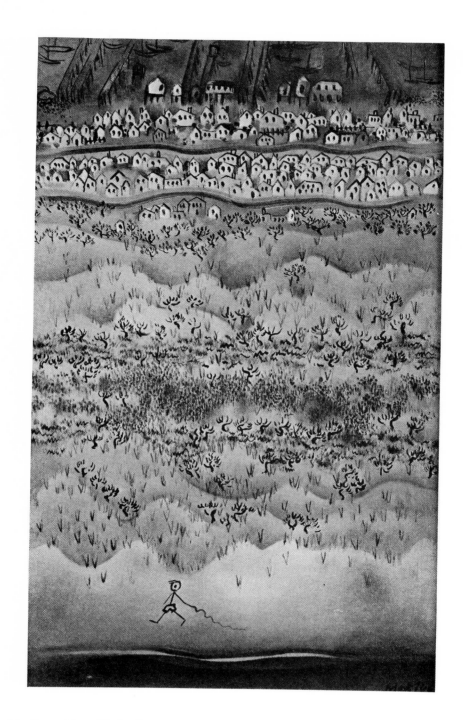

92 Loren MacIver, New York: Dune Landscape

93 Austin Mecklem, New York: Skiers

95 Hester Miller Murray, Illinois: Buffalo at Night

94 Roland Mousseau, New York: Landscape

101 Gregorio Prestopino, New York: American Landscape

97 Jane Ninas, Louisiana: Negro Cemetery

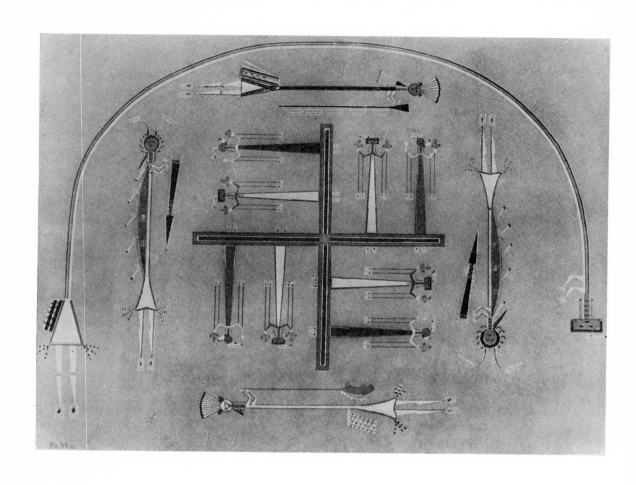

103 Red Robin, Colorado: Hasjelti Dailjis, sand painting

110 Manuel Tolegian, New York: Pennsylvania Landscape

111 Eugene Trentham, Colorado: Golden, Colorado

116 Arnold Wiltz, New York: Bridge and Dam

118 Edgar Yaeger, Michigan: Still Life

115 Frede Vidar, New York: Pool

124 Cameron Booth, Minnesota: Street in Stillwater

123 Rainey Bennett, Illinois: Storm Threat

126 Raymond Breinin, Illinois: Landscape

129 Bob Brown, Minnesota: Ashes

130 Samuel J. Brown, Pennsylvania: Mrs. Simmons

133 Glenn Chamberlain, Iowa: Landscape

139　Carlos Dyer, California: Palos Verdes Landscape

134 Joseph De Mers, California: Post No Bills

137   Helen Blackmur Dickson, Massachusetts: Fisherman's Shack

140 Stuart Edie, New York: Red Table

144 Thomas Flavell, Pennsylvania: The Station

141 Stanford Fenelle, Minnesota: Road

150 Jack Greitzer, Ohio: Memory

147   Oronzo Gasparo, New York: Promenade

148 Isolde Therese Gilbert, Massachusetts: Millbridge Road

152 Edward Lewandowski, Wisconsin: Lobster Markers

164 Lester Schwartz, Illinois: Circus Day

162 Andrée Rexroth, California: San Francisco Bay

155 Ann Michalov, Illinois: Approaching Storm

165 William Earl Singer, Illinois: Little Immigrant

171 John Stenvall, Illinois: Ohio River Flood

166 William Sommer, Ohio: Ordering Lunch

178 Elizabeth Terrell, New York: Red Still Life

186 Karl Zerbe, Massachusetts: Houses on the River

182 Joseph Vavak, Illinois: The Dispossessed

GRAPHIC ARTS

228 Hugh Miller, New York: Machinery

193 Jolan Gross Bettelheim, Ohio: "Unemployed" Office

203   Horatio C. Forjohn, Pennsylvania: Confusion at 40

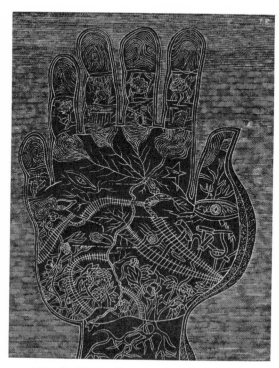

192   F. G. Becker, New York: John Henry's Hand

239 Julius Weiss, New York: Windows

216 Eli Jacobi, New York: All Night Mission

SCULPTURE

245　Patrocino Barela, New Mexico: Holy Family

241 Patrocino Barela, New Mexico: The Coronation of the Virgin

249 Samuel Cashwan, Michigan: Reclining Nude

256 Concetta Scaravaglione, New York: Girl with Fawn

254 Hugo Robus, New York: Dog: sculpture for children's playground,
First Houses, New York City Housing Project

Children's playground with animal sculptures: First Houses, New York City Housing Project

ALLIED ARTS

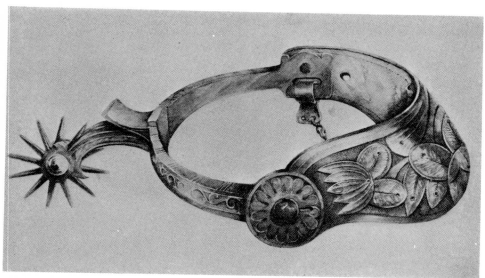

Index of American Design
265 California: Spanish-Californian spur, c. 1852

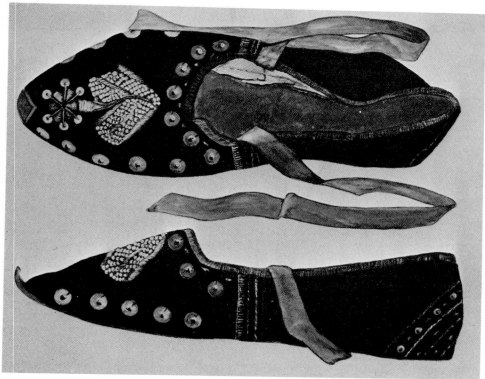

Index of American Design
258 California: slipper, c. 1820

Index of American Design
340 New Mexico: Bulto, 1810-50

Index of American Design
344 New Mexico: painted pine chest

Index of American Design
311   Massachusetts: Shaker sill cupboard, c. 1810

Index of American Design
302   Massachusetts: Shaker dairy counter, 1876

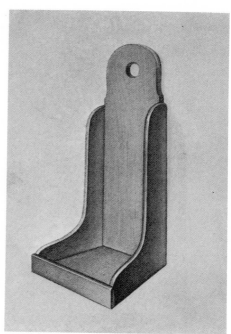

Index of American Design
306 Massachusetts: Shaker candle sconce, 1800-50

Index of American Design
329 Massachusetts: Shaker loom stool, c. 1830

Index of American Design
349 New York: Iron deer weather-vane

Index of American Design
357 New York: Cornhusk doll

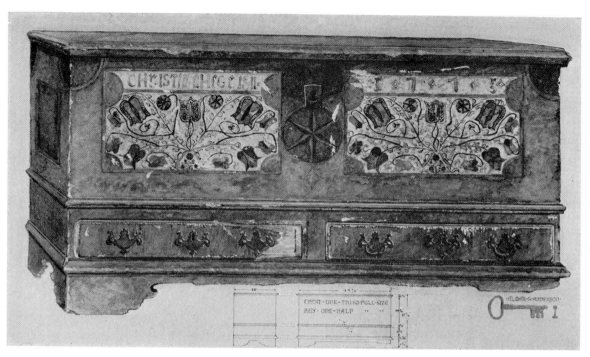

Index of American Design
365 Pennsylvania: painted chest, 1775

Index of American Design
366 Pennsylvania: pie plate, c. 1800

Index of American Design
356 New York: Patchwork quilt

Index of American Design
315 Massachusetts: chair-seat, 17th century

384 Katherine Milhous, Pennsylvania: Poster

385 Katherine Milhous, Pennsylvania: Poster

388 Hester Miller Murray, Illinois: Poster for zoo

CHILDREN'S WORK

392 Mick Arsena, aged 16, New York: Politics under the "El"

420 Louis Novar, aged 14, New York: The Butcher

395 Alphonso Basile, aged 13, District of Columbia: Robinson Crusoe as a Young Man

407 Isaiah Eisen, aged 12, New York: Boiler Menders

430 Hyman Dorfman, aged 14, New York: Mother and Child

417 Joe Larkin, aged 12, Connecticut: The Nativity

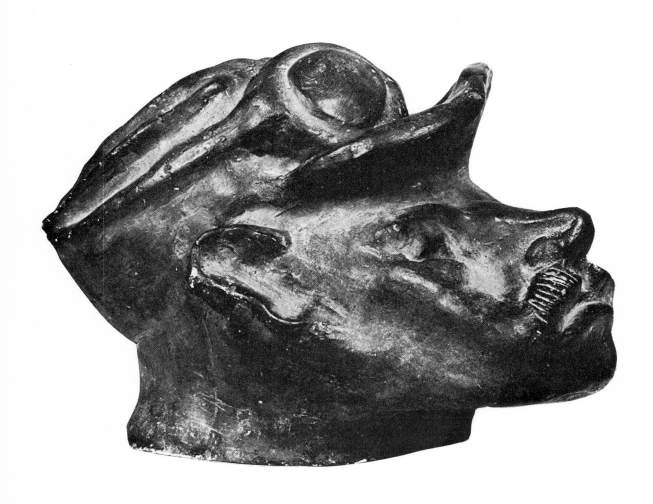

434 Mike Mosco, aged 15, New York: Miner

422 F. Rick, aged 10, New York: Passover Feast

400 Alfredo Casale, aged 10, New York: Interior

CATALOG OF THE EXHIBITION

Catalog items preceded with · are illustrated by a plate which bears the same number.

MURAL PROJECT

CHARLES ALSTON. Born 1907.   New York

Mystery and Magic Contrasted with Modern Science and Medicine: *two panels in entrance lobby of Women's Wing, Harlem Hospital, New York. Oil on canvas, 250 square feet.*

1   Color study for one panel

2   Full-sized detail, *oil on canvas*

FRANCES AVERY. Born 1910.   New York

Maternity or the History of Obstetrics: *series of panels on four walls of doctors' library, Lincoln Hospital, Bronx. Oil on canvas, 690 square feet.*

3   Detail, *watercolor*

RAINEY BENNETT. Born 1907.   Illinois

Series of eight panels for Crippled Boys' Ward, Research and Educational Hospitals, University of Illinois Medical Unit, Chicago.

4   Watercolor study for one panel: Apple Harvest and Farm Animals

5   Completed panel: Birds and Quiet Animals, *oil on canvas*

LUCIENNE BLOCH. Born 1909.   New York

The Cycle of a Woman's Life: *panel in recreation room, House of Detention for Women, New York. Fresco, 119 square feet.*

6   Photograph of finished panel

EDGAR BRITTON. Born 1901.   Illinois

Classroom Studies and Their Application: *six panels in entrance hall of Bloom Township High School, Chicago Heights. Fresco.*

7   Detail, *egg tempera on board*

· 8   Photographs of completed panels

JAMES BROOKS. Born 1906.   New York

Acquisition of Long Island: *panel in Woodside Branch Library, Long Island. Tempera on gesso, 180 square feet.*

9   Model showing interior with mural

MURAL PROJECT

ALFRED CRIMI. Born 1900.   New York

Preventive Medicine and Surgery: *panel in Medical Board Conference Room, Harlem Hospital, New York. Fresco, 250 square feet.*

  10 Color study

  11 Cartoon

  12 Full-sized detail, *fresco*

· 13 Photograph of completed panel

WYATT DAVIS. Born 1906.   New York

Mechanical Aspects of Airplane Construction: *photo-mural in Administration Building, Newark Airport, New Jersey. Photo-montage, 204 square feet.*

· 14 Photograph of study

PHILIP EVERGOOD. Born 1901.   New York

The Story of Richmond Hill: *three panels on one wall of reference room, Richmond Hill Branch Library, Richmond Hill, Long Island. Oil on canvas, 160 square feet.*

  15 Color study

  16 Model showing interior with mural

  17 Photograph of completed mural

SEYMOUR FOGEL. Born 1911.   New York

Music, Classic and Primitive: *two panels in music room of Abraham Lincoln High School, Brooklyn. Oil on canvas, 350 square feet.*

  18 Color study of one panel

  19 Section of cartoon

ARSHILE GORKY. Born 1904.   New York

Aviation: Evolution of Forms under Aerodynamic Limitations: *ten panels in second floor foyer, Administration Building, Newark Airport, New Jersey. Oil on canvas, 1530 square feet.*

    20 One completed panel, *oil on canvas*

    21 Model showing interior with murals

    22 Photographs of largest panels

RALF HENRICKSEN. Born 1907.   Illinois
    The Elements: *four panels in Gordon School, Lake Forest, Illinois. Oil on canvas.*

  · 23 Watercolor study for two panels: Earth and Water

EMANUEL JACOBSON. Born 1907.   Illinois
    Series of panels for Horace Mann School, Oak Park, Illinois. Oil on canvas.

  · 24 Watercolor study for one panel: Early Schoolroom

    25 Watercolor study for one panel: Early Living room

    Transportation: *panel for Elgin State Hospital, Chicago. Oil on canvas.*

    26 Watercolor study

    Philo Carpenter, Chicago's First Pharmacist; *panel for University of Illinois School of Pharmacy, Chicago. Oil on canvas.*

    27 Watercolor study

EDWIN BOYD JOHNSON. Born 1904.   Illinois
    Medical Pioneers: *series of panels for main library, University of Illinois College of Medicine, Chicago. Fresco.*

  · 28 Photographs

KARL KELPE. Born 1898.   Illinois
    Pioneer Days: *two panels in Hawthorne School, Oak Park, Illinois. Oil on canvas.*

    29 Watercolor study: Early Settlers

    30 Watercolor study: Early Farmers

    31 Photograph of completed panel: Early Settlers

  · 32 Photograph of completed panel: Early Farmers

DMITRI KESSEL. Born 1902. New York

Symbols of Aviation: *photo-mural for first floor of Administration Building, Newark Airport, New Jersey.*

33 Photograph of study

KARL KNATHS. Born 1891. Massachusetts

Music: *series of panels in music room of Falmouth High School, Falmouth, Massachusetts. Oil on canvas.*

34 Color studies

· 35 Photographs of completed panels

BENJAMIN KNOTTS. Born 1898. New York
GUY MacCOY. Born 1905.

Decorative Map of the World: *panel in fourth floor corridor of Julia Richman High School, New York. Oil on canvas, 2000 square feet.*

36 Photographs of completed panel

EDWARD LANING. Born 1906. New York

Rôle of the Immigrant in the Industrial Development of America: *seventeen panels in main dining room, Administration Building, Ellis Island. Tempera on canvas.*

37 Pencil studies

ABRAHAM LISHINSKY. Born 1905. New York

Major Influences in Civilization: *twelve panels in auditorium of Samuel Tilden High School, Brooklyn. Oil on canvas, 820 square feet.*

38 Black and white studies

39 Section of cartoon

ERIC MOSE. Born 1906. New York

Power: *three panels in main library of Samuel Gompers High School, Bronx. Tempera on gesso, 600 square feet.*

40 Model showing interior with murals

HESTER MILLER MURRAY. Born 1903. Illinois

Three panels in Irving School, Oak Park, Illinois. Oil on canvas.

141

MURAL PROJECT

41 Tempera study for one panel: World of Children

· 42 Photograph of completed panel: World of Children

43 Watercolor study for one panel: Animals

JAMES MICHAEL NEWELL. Born 1900. New York

Evolution of Western Civilization: *five panels in main reading room of library, Evander Childs High School, Bronx. Fresco, 1400 square feet.*

· 44 Photographs of two completed panels

45 Model showing interior with murals

WILLIAM C. PALMER. Born 1906. New York

Development of Medicine: *four panels in Incoming and Outgoing Patients' Room, Queens County General Hospital, Long Island City. Oil on canvas, 300 square feet.*

46 Full-sized detail, *oil on canvas*

47 Photograph of one completed panel

ANATOL SHULKIN. Born 1899. New Jersey

Historical and Social Function of the Court: *four panels for main entrance lobby of courthouse, Morristown, New Jersey. Fresco or oil on canvas.*

· 48 Color study, *tempera*

MITCHELL SIPORIN. Born 1910. Illinois

Prairie Poets: *proposed fresco*

· 49 Study, *egg tempera*

Children of American Literature: *proposed fresco*

50 Study, *egg tempera*

MAX SPIVAK. Born 1906. New York

Puppets: *nine panels in downstairs playroom of Astoria Branch Library, Long Island City. Oil on canvas, 260 square feet.*

· 51 One completed panel, *oil on canvas*

52 Studies in color and in ink

53 Model showing interior with murals

142

ELIZABETH TRACY. Born 1911.   Massachusetts

The Settlement of Saugus: panel in courthouse, Saugus, Massachusetts. Oil on canvas.

54 Photograph of completed panel

JOHN WALLEY. Born 1910.   Illinois

Indian Drama: stage curtain for auditorium of Lane Technical High School, Chicago.

55 Color study, *gouache and charcoal*

WILLIAMSBURG FEDERAL HOUSING PROJECT, Brooklyn, New York.

Series of proposed murals by group of eleven New York artists for social rooms of each housing unit.

56 Chart showing general housing plan, location of social rooms and index of artists

57 Model showing one housing unit with murals by Stuart Davis and Paul Kelpe

ILYA BOLOTOWSKY. Born 1907.

58 Abstraction: *color study for panel in oil on canvas, 7 by 17½ feet*

HARRY BOWDEN. Born 1907.

59 Abstraction: *color study for one of two panels in oil on canvas, 8 by 17½ and 6 by 8 feet*

BYRON BROWNE. Born 1906.

60 Abstraction: *color study for panel in oil on canvas, 9½ by 15 feet*

FRANCIS CRISS. Born 1901.

61 Abstraction: *color study for one of four panels in oil on canvas, 11 by 6 feet*

STUART DAVIS. Born 1894.

62 Abstraction: *color study for panel in oil on canvas, 14½ feet long*

MURAL PROJECT

BALCOMB GREENE. Born 1904.

> 63 Abstraction: *color study for panel in oil on canvas, 7 ½ by 11 ¾ feet*

PAUL KELPE. Born 1902.

> 64 Abstraction: *color study for panel in oil on canvas, 9½ by 11¾ feet*

WILLIAM DE KOONING. Born 1904.

> 65 Abstraction: *color study for panel in oil on canvas, 14½ by 9½ feet*

JAN MATULKA. Born 1892.

> 66 Abstraction: *color study for panel in oil on canvas, 8¼ by 7½ feet*

GEORGE McNEIL. Born 1909.

> 67 Abstraction: *color study for panel in oil on canvas, 11 by 9¾ feet*

ALBERT SWINDEN. Born 1901.

> 68 Abstraction: *color study for panel in oil on canvas, 8¼ by 11½ feet*

Models showing interiors with murals in place have been constructed under the Model Division of the Federal Art Project.

EASEL PROJECT: OIL PAINTINGS

AARON BOHROD. Born 1907.   Illinois

> 69 Landscape in Winter, *oil on composition board*

PEDRO CERVANTEZ. Born 1915.   New Mexico

> · 70 Croquet Ground, *oil on composition board*

ALLAN ROHAN CRITE. Born 1910.   Massachusetts

> 71 School's Out, *oil on canvas*

EASEL PROJECT: OIL PAINTINGS

STUART DAVIS. Born 1894.   New York
    72 Waterfront, *oil on canvas*

JOSEPH DE MARTINI. Born 1896.   New York
    · 73 Moonlight, *oil on canvas*

EMMET EDWARDS. Born 1906.   New York
    · 74 Abstraction, *oil on canvas*

DONALD FORBES. Born 1905.   New York
    75 Millstone, *oil on canvas*

KARL FORTESS. Born 1907.   New York
    · 76 Winter Vista, *oil on canvas*

LEON GARLAND. Born 1896.   Illinois
    · 77 Fry Street, *oil on canvas*

HOWARD GIBBS. Born 1904.   Massachusetts
    78 Spring Landscape, *oil on canvas*

LOUIS GUGLIELMI. Born 1906.   New York
    · 79 Wedding in South Street, *oil on canvas*
    80 Hague Street, *oil on canvas*

JAMES GUY. Born 1909.   New York
    81 Sheriff's Sale, *oil on canvas*

MARSDEN HARTLEY. Born 1877.   New York
    82 Tropic Fantasy, *oil on canvas*

HILAIRE HILER. Born 1898.   California
    83 San Francisco Street, *oil on board*

LEON KELLY. Born 1901.   Pennsylvania
    · 84 Setting the Table, *oil on canvas*

GEORGINA KLITGAARD. Born 1893.   New York
    85 Oyster Boat, *oil on canvas*

145

EASEL PROJECT: OIL PAINTINGS

KARL KNATHS. Born 1891.   Massachusetts
    86 Duck Decoy, *oil on canvas*

LAWRENCE LEBDUSKA. Born 1894.   New York
    · 87 Farm Team, *oil on canvas*

JULIAN LEVI. Born 1900.   New York
    88 Demolished Lighthouse, *oil on canvas*

JACK LEVINE. Born 1914.   Massachusetts
    89 Card Game, *oil on composition board*
    · 90 Conference, *oil on canvas*

WILLIAM LITTLEFIELD. Born 1902.   Massachusetts
    · 91 Fantasy of a Fire and Figure, *oil on canvas*

LOREN MacIVER. Born 1909.   New York
    · 92 Dune Landscape, *oil on canvas*

AUSTIN MECKLEM. Born 1894.   New York
    · 93 Skiers, *oil on canvas*

ROLAND MOUSSEAU. Born 1889.   New York
    · 94 Landscape, *oil on canvas*

HESTER MILLER MURRAY. Born 1903.   Illinois
    · 95 Buffalo at Night, *egg tempera*

JOHN NICHOLS. Born 1899.   New York
    96 Buzz Saw, *oil on canvas*

JANE NINAS. Born 1913.   Louisiana
    · 97 Negro Cemetery, *oil on canvas*

HENRY ALLEN NORD. Born 1904.   California
    98 Our Daily Interests, *oil on gesso panel*

JOSEPH PANDOLFINI. Born 1908.   New York
    99 Vegetable Still Life, *oil on canvas*

EASEL PROJECT: OIL PAINTINGS

IGOR PANTUHOFF. Born 1911.   New York
    100 Ventilator, *oil on canvas*

GREGORIO PRESTOPINO.   New York
    ·101 American Landscape, *oil on gesso board*
    102 Green Mountain Village, *oil on canvas*

RED ROBIN. Born 1910.   Colorado
    ·103 Hasjelti Dailjis, *sand painting*

MISHA REZNIKOFF. Born 1905.   New York
    104 New York, *oil on composition board*

WILLIAM SCHWARTZ. Born 1896.   Illinois
    105 Village Square, *oil on canvas*

CHARLES SEBREE. Born 1912.   Illinois
    106 Two Boats, *oil on canvas*

CLAIRE SILBER.   Louisiana
    107 Napoleon Docks, *oil on canvas*

JOSEPH STELLA. Born 1880.   New York
    108 Bridge, *oil on canvas*

ELIZABETH TERRELL. Born 1908.   New York
    109 Still Life on a Footstool, *oil on canvas*

MANUEL TOLEGIAN. Born 1912.   New York
    ·110 Pennsylvania Landscape, *tempera with
          oil glaze on gesso board*

EUGENE TRENTHAM. Born 1912.   Colorado
    ·111 Golden, Colorado, *oil on canvas*

BUMPEI USUI. Born 1898.   New York
    112 Coal Barges, *oil on canvas*

DOROTHY VARIAN. Born 1895.   New York
    113 Portrait of Eugenice, *oil on canvas*

EASEL PROJECT: OIL PAINTINGS

JOSEPH VAVAK.   Born 1891.   Illinois
    114   The Flood, *oil on canvas*

FREDE VIDAR.   Born 1911.   New York
    · 115   Pool, *oil on canvas*

ARNOLD WILTZ.   Born 1889.   New York
    · 116   Bridge and Dam, *oil on canvas*

ROBERT WOOLSEY.   Born 1913.   California
    117   Early Morning, *oil on canvas*

EDGAR YAEGER.   Born 1900.   Michigan
    · 118   Still Life. *oil on canvas*

KARL ZERBE.   Born 1903.   Massachusetts
    119   Beacon Hill, *oil on canvas*

EASEL PROJECT: WATERCOLORS, GOUACHES, PASTELS

CHARLES BARROWS.   Born 1903.   New Mexico
    120   Snow on the Mountains, *watercolor*
    121   Sunlight on the Rio Grande, *watercolor*

RAINEY BENNETT.   Born 1907.   Illinois
    122   Garden Entrance, *watercolor*
    · 123   Storm Threat, *watercolor*

CAMERON BOOTH.   Born 1892.   Minnesota
    · 124   Street in Stillwater, *gouache*
    125   The Bridge, *gouache*

RAYMOND BREININ.   Born 1909.   Illinois
    126   Landscape, *gouache*
    127   Lonesome Farm, *gouache*

LESTER BRIDAHAM.   Born 1899.   Massachusetts
    128   Men Digging in a Hill, *watercolor*

EASEL PROJECT: WATERCOLORS, GOUACHES, PASTELS

BOB BROWN.   Born 1895.   Minnesota
  · 129 Ashes, *watercolor*

SAMUEL J. BROWN.   Born 1907.   Pennsylvania
  · 130 Mrs. Simmons, *watercolor*
    131 Child Prodigy, *watercolor*
    132 The Writing Lesson, *watercolor*

GLENN CHAMBERLAIN.   Born 1914.   Iowa
  · 133 Landscape, *watercolor*

JOSEPH DE MERS.   Born 1910.   California
  · 134 Post No Bills, *watercolor*
    135 House across the Street, *watercolor*
    136 Suburb, *watercolor*

HELEN BLACKMUR DICKSON.   Born 1906.   Massachusetts
  · 137 Fisherman's Shack, *watercolor*
    138 Landscape, *watercolor*

CARLOS DYER.   Born 1906.   California
  · 139 Palos Verdes Landscape, *watercolor*

STUART EDIE.   Born 1908.   New York
  · 140 Red Table, *tempera*

STANFORD FENELLE.   Born 1909.   Minnesota
  · 141 Road, *gouache*
    142 Homing Pigeons in a Storm, *gouache*
    143 Farm with Pines, *gouache*

THOMAS FLAVELL.   Born 1906.   Pennsylvania
  · 144 The Station, *pastel*
    145 Pennsylvania Farmhouse, *pastel*
    146 Factory by the River, *pastel*

EASEL PROJECT: WATERCOLORS, GOUACHES, PASTELS

ORONZO GASPARO. Born 1903.   New York
  · 147 Promenade, *gouache*

ISOLDE THERESE GILBERT. Born 1907.   Massachusetts
  · 148 Millbridge Road, *watercolor*

ALBERT GOLD. Born 1906.   Rhode Island
  149 Head, *oil on paper*

JACK GREITZER. Born 1910.   Ohio
  · 150 Memory, *watercolor*

JULIAN LEVI. Born 1900.   New York
  151 Jersey Shore, *watercolor*

EDWARD LEWANDOWSKI. Born 1914.   Wisconsin
  · 152 Lobster Markers, *watercolor*
  153 River Tug, *watercolor*

RICHARD MERRICK. Born 1903.   Florida
  154 Barroom, *watercolor*

ANN MICHALOV. Born 1904.   Illinois
  · 155 Approaching Storm, *watercolor*

HESTER MILLER MURRAY. Born 1903.   Illinois
  156 Pipestone Lake, *watercolor*

LOUIS NISANOFF. Born 1907.   New York
  157 Filling Station, *oil on paper*

GLENN PEARCE. Born 1912.   Pennsylvania
  158 Winter Idyll, *watercolor*

ALBERT PEARSON. Born 1911.   Illinois
  159 Cow Barn, *watercolor*

GEORGE POST. Born 1906.   California
  160 Aquatic Park, *watercolor*

EASEL PROJECT: WATERCOLORS, GOUACHES, PASTELS

ARNOLD PYLE. Born 1908.   Iowa
   161 The Derelict, *watercolor*

ANDRÉE REXROTH. Born 1902.   California
  ·162 San Francisco Bay, *watercolor*
   163 Night Sky, *watercolor*

LESTER SCHWARTZ. Born 1912.   Illinois
  ·164 Circus Day, *gouache*

WILLIAM EARL SINGER. Born 1909.   Illinois
  ·165 Little Immigrant, *watercolor*

WILLIAM SOMMER. Born 1867.   Ohio
  ·166 Ordering Lunch, *watercolor*
   167 The Round Table, *watercolor*
   168 Peaches in Glass, *watercolor*
   169 Arrangement III, *watercolor*
   170 Arrangement IV, *watercolor*

JOHN STENVALL. Born 1907.   Illinois
  ·171 Ohio River Flood, *watercolor*
   172 Street, *watercolor*

ELINOR STONE. Born 1912.   California
   173 In Hooverville, *pastel*

FRANCES STRAIN. Born 1898.   Illinois
   174 Winter Landscape, *watercolor*

RICHARD SUSSMAN. Born 1908.   New York
   175 Farm Scene, *watercolor*

RUFINO TAMAYO. Born 1901.   New York
   176 Waiting Woman, *watercolor*
   177 Monday, *watercolor*

EASEL PROJECT: WATERCOLORS, GOUACHES, PASTELS

ELIZABETH TERRELL.   Born 1908.   New York
  · 178 Red Still Life, *tempera*
   179 Fruit, *tempera*

DAVID VAN RAALTE.   Born 1909.   New York
   180 Coal Yard, *watercolor*

JOSEPH VAVAK.   Born 1891.   Illinois
   181 Dust Storm, *watercolor*
  · 182 The Dispossessed: Contemporary History, *watercolor*
   183 Winter Scene, *watercolor*

FREDE VIDAR.   Born 1911.   New York
   184 Washington Square, *gouache*

JOHN WALLEY.   Born 1910.   Illinois
   185 Start of the Wild Horse Race, *watercolor*

KARL ZERBE.   Born 1903.   Massachusetts
  · 186 Houses on the River, *gouache*
   187 Winter Morning on the Square, *gouache*

GRAPHIC ARTS PROJECT

MAXINE ALBRO.   Born 1900.   California
   188 American Indian Pottery, *colored lithograph*

GIUSEPPE AMATO.   Born 1863.   Illinois
   189 From My Window, *pencil drawing*

RALPH AUSTIN.   Born 1912.   California
   190 Barbary Coast, *lithograph*

CHARLES BARROWS.   Born 1903.   New Mexico
   191 Chimayo Church, *oil smudge*

F. G. BECKER.   Born 1913.   New York
  · 192 John Henry's Hand, *wood engraving*

JOLAN GROSS BETTELHEIM. Born 1902. Ohio
  · 193 "Unemployed" Office, *lithograph*
  194 Factory Houses, *lithograph*

ARNOLD BLANCH. Born 1896. New York
  195 The Cornfield, *lithograph*

JULIUS BLOCH. Born 1888. Pennsylvania
  196 Dead Soldier, *lithograph*
  197 "Ole Man", *charcoal drawing*

REDMOND BYRON. Born 1890. California
  198 Union Square, San Francisco, *lithograph*

GEORGE CONSTANT. Born 1892. New York
  199 George Washington Bridge, *drypoint*

HUBERT DAVIS. Born 1902. New York
  200 Trees at Night, *lithograph*
  201 Desplaines River, *lithograph*

MABEL DWIGHT. Born 1876. New York
  202 Museum Guard, *lithograph*

HORATIO C. FORJOHN. Born 1911. Pennsylvania
  · 203 Confusion at 40, *air brush*
  204 Traffic Control, *air brush*
  205 Stratosphere Flight, *air brush*
  206 Idle Governor, *air brush*

EMIL GANSO. Born 1895. New York
  207 Still Life, *wood engraving*

CHARLES R. GARDNER. Born 1901. Pennsylvania
  208 Mixer, Paper Mill, *wood engraving*
  209 Paper Making, *wood engraving*

GRAPHIC ARTS PROJECT

HARRY GOTTLIEB. Born 1895.   New York
    210 Three-lane Traffic, *lithograph*

BLANCHE GRAMBS. Born 1916.   New York
    211 Dock Scene, East River, *lithograph*

JOHN W. GREGORY. Born 1903.   Massachusetts
    212 Night in Provincetown, *wood engraving*

NILS GREN. Born 1893.   California
    213 Silent Men, *lithograph*

JOHN P. HEINS. Born 1896.   New York
    214 Flowers, *linoleum cut*

RICHARD HOOD. Born 1910.   Pennsylvania
    215 Gossip, *etching*

ELI JACOBI. Born 1898.   New York
    · 216 All Night Mission, *linoleum cut*
    217 Bar and Grill, *linoleum cut*

GENE KLOSS. Born 1903.   New Mexico
    218 Rio Grande Pueblo, *etching*

YASUO KUNIYOSHI. Born 1893.   New York
    219 Landscape, *pencil drawing*

LAWRENCE KUPFERMAN. Born 1909.   Massachusetts
    220 Beacon Hill Mansion, *etching*

LUCIEN LABAUDT. Born 1880.   California
    221 False Dimension, *lithograph*

BLANCHE LAZZELL. Born 1878.   Massachusetts
    222 My Wharf Studio, *color woodcut*

CHARLES LOCKE. Born 1899.   New York
    223 In the Park, *etching and engraving*

NAN LURIE. Born 1910.   New York
   224 Women's House of Detention, *lithograph*

KYRA MARKHAM. Born 1891.   New York
   225 The Flies at Minsky's, *lithograph*

JAMES MARSHALL. Born 1906.   Utah
   226 Evil Eye, *lithograph*

HUGH MILLER. Born 1911.   New York
   227 Head, *lithograph*
   · 228 Machinery, *lithograph*

ARTHUR MURPHY. Born 1906.   California
   229 Horses, California, *lithograph*

M. LOIS MURPHY. Born 1901.   New York
   230 Fish Day, *woodcut*

CHARLES E. PONT. Born 1898.   New York
   231 Burning of the Oquendo, 1898, *wood engraving*

ANTON REFREGIER. Born 1905.   New York
   232 Mine Accident, *linoleum cut*

DOROTHY RUTKA. Born 1907.   Ohio
   233 Conference, *aquatint*

RAYMOND SKOLFIELD. Born 1909.   New York
   234 New York Harbor, *lithograph*

RAPHAEL SOYER. Born 1899.   New York
   235 Back Stage, *etching*

HARRY STERNBERG. Born 1904.   New York
   236 Night Flight, *aquatint*

WILLIAM H. TRAHER. Born 1911.   Colorado
   237 Early Irrigation Methods, Colorado, *charcoal study
      for color lithograph*

GRAPHIC ARTS PROJECT

JOSEPH VOGEL. Born 1911.   New York
  238 Pier, *lithograph*

JULIUS WEISS. Born 1912.   New York
  · 239 Windows, *scratchboard*
  240 Scene in the Park, *scratchboard*

SCULPTURE PROJECT

PATROCINO BARELA. Born 1908.   New Mexico
  Wood carvings, native pine:
  · 241 The Coronation of the Virgin
  242 The Ten Commandments
  243 God the Father
  244 The Twelve Apostles
  · 245 Holy Family
  246 Santo Nino
  247 Hope or the Four Stages of Man
  248 Heavy Thinker

SAMUEL CASHWAN. Born 1900.   Michigan
  · 249 Reclining Nude, *stone*

EUGENIE GERSHOY. Born 1902.   New York
  250 Puppet: *figure for downstairs playroom of Astoria Branch Library, Long Island City. Painted plaster*

AARON GOODELMAN. Born 1890.   New York
  251 Homeless, *plaster*

JOSE RUIZ DE RIVERA. Born 1904.   New York
  252 Bird Form: *carved metal model for monument for Newark Airport, New Jersey*
  253 Abstraction: *plaster model for stone sculpture for Williamsburg Federal Housing Project, Brooklyn*

156

SCULPTURE PROJECT

HUGO ROBUS. Born 1885.   New York
·254 Dog: *plaster model for cast cement sculpture for children's playground at First Houses, New York City Housing Project*

FINGAL ROSENQUIST. Born 1901.   Pennsylvania
255 Mother and Child, *cast stone*

CONCETTA SCARAVAGLIONE. Born 1900.   New York
·256 Girl with Fawn, *plaster*
257 Girl Reading, *terra cotta. Designed for Evander Childs High School, Bronx*

ALLIED ARTS PROJECT: INDEX OF AMERICAN DESIGN

CALIFORNIA   Drawings by Ann Buckley
·258 Embroidered velvet dancing shoe, c. 1840
259 Embroidery, c. 1845

Drawings by Gordena Jackson
260 Iron hitching post, c. 1869
261 Wool floral wreath, c. 1876

Drawings by Bertha Semple
262 Brass powder flask, c. 1855
263-264 Gold-mounted hair jewelry, c. 1840

Drawings by Gerald Transpota
·265 Spanish-Californian spur, c. 1852
266 Spanish-Californian spur, c. 1875
267 Leather cover for baptismal font, San Buenaventura Mission, c. 1820

Drawing by Lyman Young
268 Embroidered leather scabbard, c. 1831

COLORADO   Drawings by Maude Fiorentino-Vallé
269-271 Three Spanish-Colonial santos retablos, tempera on gesso panels

ALLIED ARTS PROJECT: INDEX OF AMERICAN DESIGN

159

ALLIED ARTS PROJECT: INDEX OF AMERICAN DESIGN

ALLIED ARTS PROJECT: PHOTOGRAPHY

ALLIED ARTS PROJECT: POSTERS

EDUCATIONAL PROJECT: CHILDREN'S PAINTINGS

EDUCATIONAL PROJECT: CHILDREN'S PAINTINGS

NAOMI BAKER: Bronx House, New York.   Aged 8
   393 Hockey, *gouache*

VERA BAKER: Bronx House, New York.   Aged 8
   394 Yentas, *gouache*

ALPHONSO BASILE: Friendship House, Washington, D. C.
                                                       Aged 13
  · 395 Robinson Crusoe as a Young Man, *oil on paper*

BERIO BENEYENTO: Y.M.H.A., 110th St., New York.   Aged 10
   396 Circus Parade, *watercolor*

THOMAS BOLLELA: Catholic Boys' Club, Bronx, New York.
   397 Ten Nights in a Barroom, *watercolor*   Aged 12

A. BORROSCO: Grace Chapel, New York.   Aged 12
   398 Fruit, *gouache*

KEITH BURTON: Kalamazoo Art Institute, Kalamazoo, Michigan.
   399 Speed, *gouache*   Aged 10

ALFREDO CASALE: Jefferson Park Boys' Club, New York.
  · 400 Interior, *gouache*   Aged 10
   401 Waterfront, *gouache*

GEORGE COONEY: West Side Boys' Club, New York.   Aged 15
   402 Shoppers, *gouache*

VERNON COFFIN: Avery Memorial, Hartford, Connecticut.
   403 Still Life, *watercolor*   Aged 12

ALFRED CROWLEY: Gramercy Boys' Club, New York. Aged 11
   404 D. S. C., *oil on paper*

JAMES DOYLE: Boys' Welcome Home, New York.   Aged 12
   405 Motor Boat Race, *gouache*

P. DUBLINSKY: Educational Alliance, New York.   Aged 10
   406 A Bowl of Fruit, *gouache*

EDUCATIONAL PROJECT: CHILDREN'S PAINTINGS

ISAIAH EISEN: Council House, New York.   Aged 12
- 407 Boiler Menders, *gouache*

408 Second Avenue "El", *gouache*

REBECCA FELDMAN: Bronx House, New York.   Aged 10

409 Homework, *gouache*

YON FOOK: School of Americanization, Washington, D. C.
                             Aged 13

410 Sea and Rocks, *watercolor*

JOE GANELLO: Jefferson Park Boys' Club, New York.   Aged 14

411 The Dark, *gouache*

CLARENCE GREY: Abyssinian Baptist Church, New York.
                              Aged 12

412 Raw Vegetables, *gouache*

DOROTHY HARDIN: Norwegian Children's Home, New York.
                              Aged 10

413 Our Finny Friends, *gouache*

MARIE KLEPPE: Norwegian Children's Home, New York. Aged 11

414 Play, *watercolor*

JOAN KNOBE: Sunnyside Jewish Center, New York.   Aged 15

415 Jewish Wedding, *gouache*

SEBASTIAN LANOTTE: Hudson Guild, New York.   Aged 9

416 Deep Sea Diver, *gouache*

JOE LARKIN: Avery Memorial, Hartford, Connecticut. Aged 12
- 417 The Nativity, *pencil drawing*

DONALD LIGUORE: Boys' Welcome Home, New York. Aged 10

418 Going to Town, *watercolor*

DOLORES MARTINEZ: Y.M.H.A., 110th St., New York. Aged 10

419 A Fairy Story, *gouache*

LOUIS NOVAR: Greenwich House, New York.   Aged 14
- 420 The Butcher, *oil on paper*

EDUCATIONAL PROJECT: CHILDREN'S PAINTINGS

RHODA RICH: East Side Jewish Settlement, New York.   Aged 12
 421 Dressmakers, *gouache*

F. RICK: East Midwood Jewish Center, New York. Aged 10
 · 422 Passover Feast, *gouache*

HELEN RIMLAND: Bronx House, New York.   Aged 11
 423 Household Duties, *gouache*

LENA SAFER: East Side Jewish Settlement, New York.   Aged 12
 424 Flying Trapeze, *gouache*

ROBERT SHUBERT: Gramercy Boys' Club, New York.   Aged 11
 425 Our Street, *watercolor*

FREDERICK SMITH: Boys' Welcome Home, New York.   Aged 10
 426 Banana Split, *gouache*

DOLORES WRIGHT: Utopia Children's Home, New York.
 427 In the Street, *gouache*   Aged 6

EDUCATIONAL PROJECT: CHILDREN'S SCULPTURE

SAM BONAMICO: Henry Street Settlement, New York.   Aged 11
 428 Circus Elephant, *wood carving*

ANTONY BUA: Gramercy Boys' Club, New York. Aged 13
 429 Clown, *plaster*

HYMAN DORFMAN: Henry Street Settlement, New York.
 · 430 Mother and Child, *wood carving* Aged 14

ANTONY DE PAOLO: Gramercy Boys' Club, New York. Aged 11
 431 Buffalo, *stone carving*

SPERO KOULTUKIS: Hamilton House, New York. Aged 11
 432 Man and Wife, *plaster*

EDUCATIONAL PROJECT: CHILDREN'S SCULPTURE

TONY MADONIA: Henry Street Settlement, New York. Aged 13
433 Chinaman, *wood carving*

MIKE MOSCO: University Settlement, New York.   Aged 15
·434 Miner, *plaster*

EDUCATIONAL PROJECT: THE DESIGN LABORATORY

435 Photographs of workshop activity

INDEX TO ARTISTS IN THE EXHIBITION:
MURAL, EASEL, GRAPHIC ARTS & SCULPTURE PROJECTS

INDEX TO ARTISTS IN THE EXHIBITION:
MURAL, EASEL, GRAPHIC ARTS & SCULPTURE PROJECTS

INDEX TO ARTISTS IN THE EXHIBITION:
MURAL, EASEL, GRAPHIC ARTS & SCULPTURE PROJECTS

THREE THOUSAND COPIES OF THIS CATALOG WERE

PRINTED FOR THE TRUSTEES OF THE MUSEUM OF

MODERN ART BY THE SPIRAL PRESS · NEW YORK